Not Your Self Help Book

Shirley Watson Moon

ISBN: 978-1-7379273-3-4

Inception Publishing
Inceptionpublishing@gmail.com

Disclaimer:

This book is general in nature and for informative purposes only.

It is solely based on the author's personal experience.

It is not intended as a substitute for professional help. If you are dealing with mental health issues, please seek help. Do not be afraid to do what is best for you. We all have struggles and need support along the way. I want you healthy and healing.

You are loved and the world needs you.

Introduction

The idea for this book came by way of a text from my best friend of over 20 years. During one of our random check-in text conversations, she said, "I think you need you to write a self-help book. I really think you have a lot to offer. I know you were going back and forth with ideas, but I really think you can do it."

If I'm being honest, my first thought was "Hell No!" My stomach was beginning to form little knots of anxiety just thinking about a "self-help" book. How was I going to write a book to try to help others when I was barely helping myself?

So, I simply replied, “I wouldn’t even know where to start something like that. I feel like I’m a hot mess lol I’ll think about it though. It may be therapeutic and a great way to bring in forty.”

I know you’re probably thinking, “Why are you telling me this? I’m trying to see how you are going to help me not be a hot mess anymore.” But what she says next is the reason this book even exists. “I don’t believe you’re a hot mess. You’ve been through a lot, and you still continue to smile. You still continue to push. Just give it a try one day. I think it would come to you easily.”

Easy, it was not but it did allow me to take a really good look at myself. The real me. The hot mess me. And by looking at me, I saw so many of you. The one who gets up every day and makes it happen. The one who fights secret battles on your own. The one who has gone through hell and back, but you still continue to smile.

Remember that smile. That smile saved my life, and who knows, it just might save yours.

The "Strong" One

How many times have you heard "You are the strongest person I know" or "If anybody can get through this, it would be you." Too many to count, right? Pat yourself on the back. Give yourself a high five. Or whatever you do to celebrate you. My celebration of choice usually involves wine but hey, let's celebrate.

Let's celebrate always having to get through things. Let's celebrate being able to shoulder all the burdens in life. Let's celebrate how much we continue to carry even when our bodies are clearly broken. Let's celebrate the title that we've earned through our blood, sweat, and tears and wear proudly as a badge of honor. "The Strong One."

Still feel like celebrating? Probably not. So why do we allow others to celebrate for us? Listen, as a proud member of "The Strong One" society, there is power in your strength but that is not all that you are. Your strength should act as a complement to all the other amazing qualities that make you who you are.

Yes, I am strong, but my body is tired, so I stayed in bed until noon on a Saturday. Yes, I can handle the hard stuff, but I don't want to handle this right now. Yes, I can get through anything but maybe I don't want to just get through it. What if I want to go through it? To feel it? To learn from it? To grow because of it? This is power.

Strength is the 25-year-old you gulping down drinks all night and you're still standing. Power is the 40-year-old you, knowing you can gulp down drinks all night and still be standing, but you remember the hangover or bad decisions that came along with it, so you decide to chill.

Strength is me writing a self-help book, telling all my sob stories to strangers so everyone can see my "Strong One" badge.

Power is me saying this road has not been easy, although I make it look damn good. I’ve dealt with things that I never wanted to talk about and things that I’ve tried to keep hidden. I’ve had days where I wanted to end it all because the heaviness was too much too bear, but through it all, I continued to smile.

Strength vs Power. I choose power.

The "Abandoned" One

Of all the pieces of my story that I've had to write, this one was the hardest. The foundation of the wall I would spend years of my life building started with this one brick. The beginning and the end.

I was always so jealous of the relationships that I saw other women have with their mothers, grandmothers, aunts, etc. I had some of those women in my life, but growing up, those relationships left a lot to be desired. The women in your life are supposed to guide you into womanhood. Show you how to embrace your femininity and empower you. All I got from mine were trust issues, people pleasing, lack of emotional intimacy, and no idea of what womanhood truly means.

My mother had her own struggles and although I forgave her, it didn't take away the pain that she caused. She was caught in a cycle of addiction and mental illness that led her to abandon her children. I can remember all the times she promised to come visit and she never came. I think of all the moments where I really needed her, and she just wasn't there. And the times she did show up, she wanted something. Whether it was a hot meal or money, she wasn't there for me. If the one person who was always supposed to be there for me could just leave, why should I expect anyone else to stick around? Why wasn't I enough?

I developed the mindset that everyone would leave me and just being little old me wasn't good enough. I struggled to make friends because I didn't trust that they wouldn't eventually see that I had nothing to offer and leave me too.

While my mother was fighting her own demons, my grandparents stepped in and took myself and my three sisters into their home. I am grateful for them because I had a decent life. I don't know what life would have been without them, but no matter how good things seemed on the outside, trauma was brewing on the inside.

My grandparents were old school. They lived by certain rules, and you had to just go with the flow. My grandmother is the sweetest woman you would ever meet but she would not hesitate to pull out her belt when I got to acting a fool. She made sure that her husband's clothes were clean and ready whenever he needed them to be. She had a hot meal ready for her family every day. She kept us dressed well and hair perfectly straight. She was at every school performance and awards ceremony. She is the wife and mother that I thought I wanted to be, until I grew up.

My grandmother was almost perfect but why did I always feel like something was missing? Was I an ungrateful, selfish brat? How could I not worship the ground that she walked on after everything that she had done for me? It's like when someone gives you a gift. What if they buy you a raincoat but you live in an area where it never rains. You appreciate the gesture and are grateful that they thought of you, but is the gift right for you? That gift was my grandmother. She did everything she thought was right, but the things she didn't do were detrimental to me.

Did any of you have a talk with your mother or other motherly figures about your period? Being optimistic here and hoping that most of you had some kind of conversation about what it meant and how it may affect you as a woman. Guess what? 'til this day I have never had a talk with any of the older women in my family about having my period or anything dealing with womanhood.

The day I started my cycle, I was at school. I was given a sanitary napkin from the nurse and sent on my way. When my dear grandmother picked me up from school that day, the basketball coach told her that I started my cycle because I had been miserable and couldn't practice that day. My grandmother went by the CVS on the way home, brought this huge pack of pads, gave me the bag and said to take a shower when I got home. That was my welcome to womanhood. If you thought that was bad, wait until you hear about my first gynecological exam.

Much like my experience having my first period, there was no discussion. I was told I had a doctor's appointment and that was it. We showed up at the office and everything seemed normal until I was called in the back. The nurse comes in and she asked me, "Do you know why you're here?" Of course, I knew why I was there. I was getting a check-up. I nod my head, yes. The nurse continues, "Well, your grandmother thinks you may be having sex and want us to make sure your safe." Y'all!! If you could have seen the look on my face!! I was dumbfounded. The only thing I knew about sex was what I managed to sneak and watch on tv or things that I heard kids at school talk about. I had just started my period about a year before and the last thing I was thinking about was sex. My darling grandmother thought that was the perfect time to excuse herself and left me in emotional turmoil with a stranger. *Insert deep breath here* To say I was hurt is an understatement. I felt ashamed, embarrassed and for some reason, dirty and I couldn't express this to anyone.

We didn't express our feelings in our house. If you were sad, you were just sad. If you had a bad day, oh well. You didn't express that to anyone. You had to figure out a way to deal with your own sadness and make your bad day better. You sweep it all under the rug with a smile. I don't ever remember hearing my grandmother tell me she loved me when I was a kid. There weren't many hugs and kisses either. There were no affirmations of how smart I am or how beautiful I was or that I could do anything and be anything, but there was plenty of "don't bring no babies in this house." Apparently, that was all they thought I could do, but I digress.

As I got older, I knew that I had trust issues due to my mother leaving but I didn't realize that my abandonment wound went much deeper than that. Yes, my mother abandoned me but so did my grandmother. She failed to provide adequate support for my development. She left me to fend for myself as woman, unable to navigate the many nuisances of womanhood and appreciate the power of my emotions. So, how do I remove this brick from my life? I don't.

Along this journey, I've learned that there are going to be some "bricks" that must be removed, while others may need to be repurposed. My greatest pain is turning into my greatest triumph. All the things I needed from the women in my life when I was a child, I give to my girls. I tell them every day how much I love them. I speak affirmations over them so that they will know that they are smart, they are kind, they are enough, they are beautiful, and that they can be whoever and whatever they want to be, but I love them just as they are. I make our home a safe space for them to express themselves. I tell them about the magic that is inside of them. I teach them how amazing it is to be a woman and when the time comes for them to enter womanhood, I will be there to celebrate them and empower them with the smile of a woman who is honored to have been chosen to guide them on their journey.

To My 5 year old self

Dearest Little One,

You are a shining star! Your laughter lights up the world, and your imagination is a magical place. You are strong, brave, and full of wonder. Know that you are deeply loved and cherished.

I'm so sorry I haven't always shown you how much I love you. You deserve to feel safe and loved every single day. I promise to work hard to make you feel that way.

Remember, you are amazing just as you are. The world is lucky to have you in it!

With all my love,
Your future self

The "Lying" One

No one wants to admit that they are a liar, especially in this world of keeping it "100" or "standing on business," but we all lie or have lied at some point in our lives. It may have been a little white lie to keep from hurting someone's feelings or a blatant lie to get something you want or to keep you out of trouble. No matter the reason, a lie is a lie.

I have always been a liar, even as a kid. I would try to lie my way out of trouble. It didn't usually work but like the saying goes, "If at first you don't succeed, try again." I kept working on my lies. Whether it was to keep me out of trouble or to get my parents to let me go somewhere, I would lie. Eventually, my lies would work and by the time I became an adult, I was pretty good at lying, but at that point, it was more than just telling a lie.

I had always been observant and could figure out how to use things to my benefit. Baby, I turned lying into an art form. I realized that one lie could get me almost anything I wanted, and I ran with it. I used to think that my lies were not intentionally hurting anyone. That they were only to make my life easier or more comfortable. I couldn't have been more wrong. My lies may not have hurt others but they damn sure hurt me.

See, every time I told a lie, it took away the opportunity for me to speak my truth. I gave away my power "to stand on business" and opted for low level tactics of weakness through lying and manipulation because I was afraid. Afraid that others may not like my opinion. Afraid of the power that comes with the truth. After all, "the truth shall set you free." And the truth was that I was afraid to be truthful because it was so much easier to live a lie.

It's hard to accept that you're a liar because no one likes a liar, but the first step to fixing a problem is admitting that you have one. I had to be honest with myself and admit that I was a liar. Even after I saw how wrong my actions were, I clung to the hope that my lies weren't as bad as others'. I justified my behavior by comparing myself to people who had caused far more damage. But deep down, I knew that wasn't right. I had to tell myself, "Girl please. You are a liar no matter how you try to spin it. Now, deal with it!" And deal with it I did.

I started to take inventory of the lies I told and why I told them. I lied about being sick to get out of work instead of just saying I needed a break. I lied to lovers about the experience being good instead of saying what I wanted or needed because I didn't want to bruise their ego. I lied about my finances because I didn't want people to pity me or judge me instead of saying I can't do it, or I don't have it right now. I lied about my feelings instead of admitting that I was upset, hurt or downright depressed because I didn't want to be seen as weak or a victim. When I realized that the lies I told only left me burdened, sexually deprived, and damn-near broke, I thought how much worse could the truth make things?

I learned to be truthful by being honest with myself. I didn't have to share every thought and opinion with the world, but I did have to be open and transparent with myself. Being honest with myself alleviated the fear and discomfort of telling the truth in those spaces where I may have lied in the past. No one else's feelings are more important than my own, and to protect their

feelings and mine, I must tell the truth. With tact
and a smile of course, and if they don't want the truth, oh well. In the infamous words of Ms. Nene Leakes, from the Real Housewives of Atlanta, "I said what I said," and I will stand on the truth any day.

To My Teenage Self

Hey you,

I know things feel overwhelming right now. You're figuring out who you are, what you believe, and where you fit in. It's confusing and scary, but you're stronger than you think.

You're going to make mistakes, have heartbreaks, and feel lost at times. That's okay. It's all part of growing up. Just remember to be kind to yourself. You're allowed to change your mind, and it's okay to not have all the answers.

Focus on building strong friendships, explore your passions, and don't be afraid to step outside your comfort zone. You're capable of amazing things.

Most importantly, know that you are loved and supported, even when it doesn't feel like it.

You've got this.

With love and encouragement,
Your future self

The "Addicted" One

H My name is Shirley and I am an addict. During my "little vacation" at Federal Prison Camp Anderson, they made everyone attend AA as a part of your release requirements. I didn't think I needed it because I wasn't an alcoholic and I didn't do drugs, but because they said I had to go, I went. It took years after my release for me to grasp the concept of my addiction. Money. I was addicted to money.

As long as I had it, I was good. I was the happiest, most generous person you would ever meet. I was helping others pay their bills, buying all kinds of gifts, treating my friends to lunch and dinner, donating to charity. I was on cloud 9. I got my “high” from having money and would do almost anything to get it, but when I didn’t have money, oh boy, it was ugly.

I had not only psychological symptoms but physical changes too. I would have headaches, tension in my neck and shoulders, and lots of stomach discomfort. I couldn’t eat or sleep until I figured out a way to put a little money in my pocket. I would go through withdrawal every time my money got low. The crazy thing is, I wasn't destitute or flat out broke. I just didn't have enough to do what I wanted when I wanted. Don't get me wrong. When I couldn't pay my bills, I would spiral into a dark place. I would experience withdrawal symptoms even after the bills were paid if I couldn't buy a new outfit for my kids or treat my family to dinner or just look at my bank account and see the money there. Eventually, I realized that my issue wasn't necessarily with money but what money represented for me.

Money to me is choices and freedom. When my money is good, I have choices. I could spend $10 on lunch or $100. I could choose the cheap nail salon or a more luxurious one. I could choose what job to take because I didn't care about the salary. I could choose the area I wanted to live in or the car I wanted to drive. With every choice also comes freedom.

The freedom to do what makes me happy. If I want to drive to the beach, I could. If I wanted a massage just because it's Monday, sign me up. Freedom from the stress of worrying about day-to-day things. Rent was always paid in advance. Never thought about lights being turned off or car getting repossessed. I could simply enjoy life and who doesn't want to enjoy life, but in order to enjoy life, I had to deal with my issues with money.

Money represented a lot to me as I was growing up. When I got good grades, I was given money or a new pair of shoes. When my parents did something wrong, they didn't apologize. They gave me money. They didn't say "I love you." It was more money or more gifts. Money was a substitute for the things I lacked. Money was ingrained in me as the most important thing in my life. My career choices should have been based on what paid well. When I got older and started toying with the idea of marriage, my grandmother's advice was "to find someone that can take care of you. You can learn to love him later." See, money was shoved at me in every aspect of my life, and I've spent my entire adult life chasing it and being obsessed with having it that I've missed out on some beautiful experiences.

I want to be able to give my girls the world, and as I continue this healing journey, the world means more than just money and things. It's giving hugs and kisses. It's getting my grown behind in a twin-sized bed with my 6-year-old because she wants to sleep with mommy. It's more movie nights and family campouts in the living room. It's breakfast for dinner and dessert for breakfast. It's telling them every day how amazing they are. It's encouraging them to follow their dreams and be true to themselves. It's all the things that money can't buy.

Now, I’m not saying that my money issues have gone away because it’s still a struggle for me sometimes, but I take it one day at a time. Celebrating how far I’ve come. Giving myself grace in those moments when I slip back into old mindsets. Enjoying the freedom from the grip of my addiction. Smiling at the amazing life I’m creating and excited to see what’s to come.

The "Giving" One

You give and you give until you can't give anymore. Everyone knows that if they need or want something, you are the one to call. You even force your giving on people who didn't ask. If you've got it, you're going to give, and I don't just mean money. You constantly give your time, your energy, your peace and yourself. You give everything to others but what are you giving to yourself?

We've all been taught that God loves a cheerful giver. So, we put on that smile and give everything we've got even at the expense of ourselves, but why do we do it? I have a few theories, but I can't speak for you. I can only speak for myself. I am one of the most giving people that I know and I truly love being able to give and help others, but when I honestly asked myself why, the answer was a bit shocking.

Like most of you, I do it from the kindness of my heart; however, I would be lying if I didn't say a bit of my ego creeps in. We all know how good it feels when we help someone, but doesn't it feel just a tiny bit better when they are appreciative of what you've done? Come on. This is a safe space. You can admit that you sometimes give because you enjoy the appreciation of the recipient more than the actual act of giving. And guess what? That's ok! I'm not telling you to be out here helping people so that you can feel superior but having a single moment where someone truly appreciates what you've done is perfectly normal. Everything is about balance.

Ah yes, balance. Does that really exist ? Is balance attainable? I’m still figuring it out, but it is definitely possible. I was the person people would call for anything and I would do it no questions asked. If you needed money and I didn’t have it, I would figure out a way to get it. If you needed a shoulder to cry on, no matter what I was going through, my shoulder was yours. If you wanted to party all night, and I had stuff I know I needed to do; I was going to party. I gave so much of myself that I had nothing left to give me. When all the money was gone and I had no more energy to give, my life was in shambles.

I gave so much and often at the expense of myself and my family. I would be struggling to maintain my household but if someone called with a need, I was going to make a way to help. Then, one day I had a wake-up call.

I was in a tough spot financially and someone very dear to me called needing some help. Y'all, I made myself sick trying to figure out what I was going to do. I prayed and meditated for days to get an answer. Well, I got an answer, and my little heart couldn't take it.

Spirit told me to stop trying to help someone else and focus on trying to help myself. I wasn't just in a tough place financially. I was physically, mentally, spiritually, and energetically "broke." I had nothing to give anybody else. Let alone myself. It was time for me to start being selfish and do what I needed to do for me. I had no problem with giving more money to myself, but it did feel a little weird.

For the first time in years, I bought bras that actually fit. I became my own shoulder to cry on by journaling more and having conversations with myself whenever I was alone (and yes, sometimes I talked backed). The hardest thing for me to give to myself was time. Between work and having a family to take care of, taking an hour or 2 for myself didn't always happen, and if I'm being truthful, it still doesn't. I give my time and energy to everyone else and have yet to figure out how to give more of it to me, but I'll get there. Writing this book was a lot of time for me so that's some progress.

Remember, “You can’t pour from an empty cup.” Make sure that your needs are met before you try to meet the needs of someone else. No one is more important than you. It’s ok to be a little selfish when it comes to making sure you’re at your best. If you’re used to operating on an empty tank, be patient with yourself. It’s not always easy to put yourself first but you’ll get there. We’ll get there. One day, and one bra, at a time.

The "Guilty" One

I'll never forget the day I stood in front of the judge and heard him say "guilty." That word echoed so loudly in my mind that everything else was a blur. Of course, I was guilty. I had accepted that but now, everyone else knew I was guilty as well. How do I move past the guilty verdict?

Some of you may relate to my courtroom experience on a

personal level, and some of you have never seen the inside of a courtroom except on tv. Nonetheless, we all have been found guilty either by a judge or by ourselves. Unfortunately for me, I was convicted by both, and the life sentence I had given myself was far worse than the 2 years, 3 months the judge gave me.

Guilt is hard because we don't always know how to turn it off. I have things that I've done that triggered feelings of guilt. I've said many things and done a lot more that have caused pain to others and in those moments, the guilt was warranted but when does it become too much?

Once I sentenced myself to a lifetime of guilt, I found myself taking a guilty plea for things that were not my cases to plea to. My boyfriend cheated on me. I didn't blame him. I blamed me because I didn't give him what he needed. I loan somebody money and they don't pay me back. I don't blame them for not keeping their word. I blamed me for not being in a better place financially so that I wouldn't need the money back. Someone is rude to me. I blamed me for whatever I may have done to cause it. Someone does something to hurt me. I blame me because I need to stop being so sensitive and get thicker skin. No matter the situation, I always found a way to make myself the guilty party.

Guilt is hard because we like to confuse it with accountability. It's one thing to accept responsibility for your actions. It's a totally different thing to be "wrong" in every situation.

Nobody is wrong all the time and you should not accept blame to spare someone else from the consequences of their actions. Guilt says, "I did something wrong and should be punished." If you are constantly telling yourself you did wrong and deserve punishment, what do you think starts to happen? You start to believe it.

When you accept guilt, you also accept the punishment. You begin to allow undesirable things in your life because you think you deserve it. I allowed abuse, infidelity, disrespect, poverty, and so much more because I felt like I deserved it. I needed to be punished because no matter what, I was always guilty.

For years that guilty verdict from the judge followed me like the stink of a skunk. I was stuck in jobs that barely paid over minimum wage. I would interview and get offers for decent jobs that on paper I qualified for, but the moment they ran the background check, denied. I was branded guilty. It took 14 years from the date I was found guilty, and sentenced, until I was able to get a job that paid over $40,000, but during those 14 years, I noticed that the effect of that guilty verdict diminished more and more. If others no longer saw that guilty verdict as a detriment to their organizations and were willing to give me a chance, then why couldn't I?

Why couldn't I allow myself to be free of the verdict that I had given myself? Yes, I may have been guilty in the past, but I shouldn't have to be punished for the rest of my life for these grievances. The hardest part of releasing myself from the guilty verdict was forgiveness. I had to forgive myself for all the things that I had done to others, the things I allowed others to do to me, and all the things that I had done to myself. It wasn't always easy, but I had to remind myself that no matter what I had done in the past, I didn't deserve a life full of pain and misery and neither do you.

We are more than our mistakes and we deserve to be given a chance. A chance to be happy. A chance to be healed. A chance to be free. By pardoning myself from that lifetime sentence, I gave myself a chance to get all the good things I deserve. Give you a chance too.

To My 20-year-old Self

Dear Past Self,

I hope this letter finds you well. I am writing to you from the future to share some insights and advice that I have gained over the years.

As you embark on this exciting journey of life, there are a few things I want you to keep in mind. Firstly, embrace the power of learning and personal growth. Never stop seeking knowledge and expanding your horizons. Be open to new experiences and challenges, and don't be afraid to step outside of your comfort zone.

Secondly, surround yourself with positive and supportive people. Choose friends and mentors who will uplift and inspire you, and who will help you become the best version of yourself.

Thirdly, be kind to yourself and practice self-compassion. There will be times when you make mistakes or face setbacks, but it's important to remember that these are all part of the learning process. Forgive yourself for your mistakes and learn from them, rather than dwelling on them.

Lastly, remember to take care of your physical and mental well-being. Make time for exercise, healthy eating, and relaxation. Prioritize your health and well-being, as they are the foundation for everything else in life.

I hope this letter serves as a reminder of your potential and the bright future that lies ahead. Embrace each day with enthusiasm and determination, and never lose sight of your dreams.

Best regards,
Your Future Self

The "Depressed" One

Before I dive into this one, let me start by saying that depression is a hell of a disease. So many of us are trying to deal with it the best way we know how. Some may experience just a bad day every now and then while others are crippled and burdened by it. No matter where you find yourself in this battle, just know you are not alone in this fight. Don't give up. The world needs you.

Less than 24 hours after giving birth to my first daughter, my battle began. I remember lying in the hospital bed and all I could do and wanted to do was cry. I brushed it off as just stress from the chaotic delivery and changing hormones of being a new mommy. I told myself, "It'll work itself out. Women have babies all the time and they're fine. You'll be fine too," but I wasn't fine. Far from it.

I shook off my "baby blues" and went on with my life. I was working, trying to be mommy, going on dates with my baby daddy (now my husband) and partying every now and then with my 2 friends. Life was fine. Yeah, I had a bad day or 30 but who didn't?

Let's fast forward about 5 years. I was newly married. My husband and I bought a condo. Our beautiful baby girl was doing amazing, and we had just welcomed a new princess into our family. I should've been on cloud nine, but I wasn't.

You see, during those five years I chose to skip, the occasional bad days had become more frequent. I had become withdrawn and couldn't fully function in the world around me. On the outside, I looked fine, but inside I had a whole storm brewing.

Slowly, my "good" life had started to unravel. My kids were becoming too much for me to handle. My husband and I were damn near enemies, and I was losing my fucking mind. I would stay in the bed for days without showering because my mind wouldn't let me. I called out of work constantly because my mind couldn't bear the thought of dealing with people. I hid myself from those that truly knew me because I didn't want them to know that something was wrong, and the few people that I didn't hide from, they didn't even notice how bad I was doing. After all, they did see me smile.

I woke up one day and I had just had enough. I was tired of pretending and feeling like a dark cloud to my husband and my kids.

I was ready to end it all. I had a doctor's appointment that morning and for some reason, I decided to go. The entire drive, all I could think about was driving my car off the road. Every time I turned the wheel to veer off the road, some outside force always pulled my car back.

I made it through my doctor's appointment and as I'm leaving to go home, a stranger stops me. The stranger looked me straight in the eye and said, "Not today. We need you," and started to walk away. After taking about 10 steps, the stranger turned around and flashed the brightest smile I had ever seen.

As I stood in the parking lot with tears rolling down my face, the stranger's words continued to echo in my mind. "Not today. We need you." When I finally made it to my car, I caught a glimpse of myself in the mirror and I noticed I was smiling but this smile was different. This was the smile of a person whose life had just been saved.

That day I decided I was going to win this battle. Most importantly, I realized that I needed help. I went to therapy. I took meds and yes, those things helped but I needed to do the work. I had to realize all the bricks that I had collected. I had to recognize how high the wall had grown. I had to be ready to tear it all down.

This journey has not been without a few twists and turns and sometimes the rumbling of depression tries to creep in. But

when it does, I remind myself that
life can be like a rollercoaster, so I
allow myself to feel the rumbling,
scream at the top of my lungs, throw
my hands up, and enjoy the ride,
with a smile of course.

The "Masculine" One

Ok, so…everything that I've discussed up until this point were things that I noticed about myself along my healing journey, but this topic was pointed out to me by someone else, my dear husband. At first, I was shocked and then offended. How dare he say that I act like a man? I'm all woman. I had 2 kids for God's sake!

And to add insult to injury, he gave me a book about femininity? A book!! Listen, when someone gives you a book about the issue, they are serious about you needing some help. We've all been handed a book at some point in our lives on how to deal with something. It could've been a book on grief, addiction, financial issues, or self-love, and when the initial attitude wears off and you reluctantly start reading it, a switch turns on in your brain. You begin to see yourself in the lines and pages of that book. I saw myself in that book. "The Black Women's Ultimate Guide to Reclaiming Femininity" by Six the

Goddis was the catalyst behind the start of this journey.

You see, I equated the superficial attributes of a woman with the undeniable energy of being feminine. I thought wearing pretty dresses and sitting with my legs crossed or hell, having breast and a vagina made me feminine. I couldn't have been more wrong.

In the book, Six says, "Decade after decade, we have proven how strong we are, we have nothing to prove anymore."

"Dysfunction has become so normal in today's society that we have begun to change our narrative to fit the dysfunction, instead of healing from it and changing our course to a healthy direction."

Healing from it. I didn't realize how dysfunctional my life was. I thought that everything was fine, and people should just accept the way that I was. Not understanding the toxicity and poison that was running through my body, was slowly killing me. I had an overload of masculine energy from having to protect myself over the years. My energy field was like Fort Knox. I be damned if I let anything in that I deemed to be a weakness, but there is nothing weak about feminine energy.

Femininity is an energy that cannot be replicated. It isn't just being a woman. It's being soft in the right moment, understanding the power of the feminine/masculine balance. It's knowing that even though you can carry the load, doesn't mean you have to. It is a power like no other. It is patient, kind and nurturing. It carries life and gives birth to nations. It supports all things and heals what is broken. It is reflected in all things beautiful. It is the twinkle in your eyes, the music in your voice, and the wind in your walk. It is your introduction when you step into a room.

"A feminine woman is more concerned about bringing a sense of balance and wit to every environment she is in as opposed to being in charge everywhere she goes." I had to learn to fall back. I didn't always have to be in charge. I could relax and trust that my husband would do what needed to be done, and I would support him along the way.

It has been a scary yet fulfilling transition. I was afraid to let my guard down. I was afraid that my daughters would view me as weak, but I was more afraid of them not knowing the true power and freedom that came with walking in their femininity. After all, I am their first teacher. I vowed to teach them to never be afraid to ask for help. I will teach them that there is power in their submission. I will teach them that when you look good, you feel good. I will teach them that being a feminine woman is awesome, and as women blessed with melanin, we rock!

The "Fearful" One

We are all afraid of something. I'm not talking about the common fears. You know-snakes, spiders, heights, etc. I'm talking about those things deep within us that we know are there but won't acknowledge. When I started writing this book, I had to face one of my hidden fears—the fear of truly being seen—allowing myself to be open and vulnerable. I wanted to share parts of myself in this book that I had never shared before, but to do that, I had to accept that I was afraid.

I couldn't just pretend that I was fine with it because I wasn't. I knew I wanted to write this book, but fear wouldn't let me. I would write a little bit and then stop for days, sometimes weeks. At first, I thought "Oh, it's just writer's block," but deep down I knew it was something more.

One day, I received a message from Spirit to write down all my fears and then to burn them as an act of release. Oh, my goodness! By the time I finished writing that list, it was 2 notebook pages long (front and back)! How the hell was I still alive and sane when I was afraid of every dam thing? I don't remember the entire list, but I know some of it was foolish things-like getting old, gaining weight, not being cute anymore-you know, real foolishness; however, the ones that truly shocked me are the ones most of us wish for the most. Success, love, and money were the biggest repetitive themes on my list of fears. Crazy, right?

How do you fear the things you spend a lifetime trying to obtain? I'll tell you how. Let's start with money. I get up every day and I go to work. My job barely pays the bills but I'm making it work. It's not difficult work and I don't hate it, so I stick with it. I'm comfortable. Sound familiar? I'm comfortable barely getting by. I would love to make more money. Who wouldn't? I started to think about all the things I could buy. The trips my family could take. The bills I could finally pay. I find myself getting excited and I begin looking for better paying jobs. Then, here comes the fear.

Now, fear can present itself in different ways among different people. For some, it can be physical symptoms-rapid heartbeat, nausea, shortness of breath, etc. For others, it can be a more mental effect-anxiety, negative thoughts, irritability, difficulty concentrating, etc.

Most of my fears affect me mentally. So, the negative thoughts and what-ifs started to creep in. "What if you get more money and you still can't pay your bills?" "What if you get more money and you're irresponsible with it?" "What if you get more money, only to lose it later and end up worse than you are now?" My favorite one, "You don't need more money. You should be grateful for what you have." Needless to say, I stopped looking for a new job and definitely wasn't thinking about any books.

Well, after having a whole breakdown and crying my eyes out in a car that was on the brink of repossession, I was over the fear. I knew I had to do something fast, but how do I change the things my brain was telling me?

For starters, I had to be honest about my situation. I was struggling and I didn't like it. I had to let go of the fake humility and even though things could be worse, I was complacent in my struggle. I was getting comfortable with almost being broke so I wasn't willing to step out to try bigger things. I started to visualize what life would be like if I had more money. The more I visualized, the more determined I was to change my situation, but how was I going to move past the fear?

That was easier said than done. For me, my fear of money was deeply rooted in past issues surrounding addiction and poor financial habits. I had to admit that I had trouble with money management, and I needed help. I had to get past the old way of thinking and start new. I set a plan for what I wanted to do with the extra money, and I always made sure that I gave myself a little fun money. I learned to stick to a budget and that it was ok to redo the budget if it wasn't working for me. I give myself grace when I slip up and know that the world isn't going to end because I want more for myself and my family. Once I realized that it wasn't a crime to have big dreams, I applied for a new job. The job was mine before the interview was even over and I now make enough to pay my bills comfortably and have a little fun on the side too.

Once I started to work on my fear of money, it made it clear why I also feared success and love. The common themes among my 3 biggest fears are mistakes and pain. I feared money because of mistakes I made in the past with it and because of it. My fear of success comes from how unworthy I felt due to past mistakes.

When I think about success, I think of the spotlight. Everything is highlighted and so bright. Everyone can see. I never wanted to be in the spotlight because I didn't want people to see certain parts of me. I didn't feel that anyone would take a convicted felon seriously. It just wasn't in the cards for me.

I was also afraid of the responsibility. “To whom much is given, much is required.” “Many are called but few are chosen.” I didn’t want to be chosen. I didn’t want to mess things up for others like I had already done for myself. I didn’t feel like I had anything to offer, but then I started to think about the people that I considered successful.

These people were not celebrities or billionaires, yet. They were people that I went to college with or people that I went to church with. These were people who followed their dreams to start their own businesses. People who have taken the journey to heal themselves physically and mentally. People who are raising amazing kids. People who live life to the fullest because tomorrow isn't promised. These people are successful to me, and if they can achieve success, why can't I? They also made mistakes, but they've moved past them and so will I.

I had to break away from the chains of my past and realize that I am already successful in my own right. I have written and published 3 books. I have sold over 100 copies of my first children's book. I have an awesome husband and the world's best daughters. I get to laugh and enjoy my life with them. I would say that my life is a success.

Once the newness of my success started to wear off, I realized that by conquering my fear of success, I also conquered my fear of love. One of my biggest accomplishments has been to love my husband and my kids without restraints or expectations. I am able to give them the love that I always wanted, but it wasn't always this way.

Love for me had always been conditional and when those conditions weren't met, it usually ended up in heartache. Over time I had built this cage around my heart, and every time something close to "love" would appear, fear would lock it out. That is until I met my husband.

It wasn't always an easy road for us because he had to deal with all the years of hurt and pain that I'd gone through, and looking back, I was unbearable at times, but he refused to give up on me. He loved me enough to walk this path with me and for that, I am so thankful. He saw past all the hurt and continued to love me anyway.

He showed me unconditional love even when it would have been easier to just walk away. He taught me what real love is and I could never go back to having anything less.

They say love conquers all and in my case, it definitely did. By letting go of the hurt and allowing myself to feel and give love, I was able to face my fears because I knew that things would only get better for me.

Think about your fears. Allow yourself to feel all the emotions surrounding those fears. Write them down. Then, release them by burning the paper. This gives your mind the ok to begin to let go. By burning them, you are affirming to yourself that you are moving past fear and stepping into triumph. Some things may linger and that's ok. Take inventory of what remains and dig deeper to see why that fear is holding on so strong.

Once you can see past your fear, you are on your way to a new path. A path of new experiences, new adventures, new goals, and new outcomes. Be ready. It's exciting up ahead and you deserve to enjoy every moment of it. You are more than any mistakes that you have made, and you are now about to experience a whole new life because you didn't allow fear to stand in your way.

The “Perfect” One

We label a lot of things as perfect. The perfect job, the perfect car, the perfect dress, the perfect spouse, but what makes these things perfect? Does the job pay well and value their employees? Does that car have all the newest features and last for years to come? Does the dress hide all the flaws while accentuating the good stuff? Does that spouse worship the ground you walk on and treat you like royalty? Yeah, these things sound great but are they really perfect?

There's an old gospel song that says, "trying to make 100 because 99 and a half won't do." It describes this vicious cycle that we find ourselves in, for a lack of a better word, perfectly. We strive for these unrealistic ideals because at some point in our lives, we have been told by ourselves or others, that we are not good enough or "just won't do." So, we push, and we push and are no closer to perfect than we were when we started. Yet, we keep going. Why?!?!

For me, it was all the years of being made to feel like I was not good enough. I wasn't pretty enough. I wasn't skinny enough. I wasn't light enough. My butt wasn't big enough. I wasn't popular enough. I wasn't friendly enough. My clothes were not expensive enough. I wasn't loud enough. I wasn't smart enough. I wasn't feminine enough. I wasn't focused enough. I wasn't wifey enough. I wasn't motherly enough. I wasn't rich enough. I wasn't me enough. I just wasn't enough, and I drove myself crazy trying to be not just enough but to be perfect.

When I look at the long list of things that I believed were not good enough, I can now laugh. I see this list for what it truly is—an unrealistic view of an imaginary standard set for me by someone who isn't living my life, and if this someone isn't living my life, how can they say when I have or haven't attained perfection? Or if I even want it?

The older I get, the more I realize that perfection does not exist. It is merely a mindset that encompasses the moment. It is that shimmer of happiness when everything else looks bleak. When your plans fall through, and you end up having the best time ever. When you give your all to a project and even though it didn't make you rich, you realize you did great work. You had this grand vision of what you expected your life to be like and although it looks different from your vision, it is exactly what you needed.

I didn't need everything to be smooth, straight lines with a place for everything and everything in its place. Don't get me wrong. I like for there to be order and neatness but sometimes, things may color a little out of the lines and that's ok with me. It doesn't rock me to my core or shake my barely holding on foundation.

I'm learning that there may be some unexpected bumps in the road and things are going to happen, but those things are not happening to me. They're just happening. I can't control everything because what fun would that be, but I will do my best with the things that I can. I will be prepared and ready for whatever may come my way. I don't have to aim for perfection anymore because in my own little way, I've already come as close as I'll ever get to whatever that may be.

The "Grateful" One

How awesome it feels to be able to say I'm grateful. There was a time in my life where I didn't always feel like I had anything to be grateful for; now, I give thanks for everything. Even the bad things or less than desirable things. As I'm writing this book, life is happening. I'm counting down to my 40th birthday, and I planned a trip for my birthday. I was gifted the funds to pay for my trip.

Amazing, right? I was so excited as financially I'm struggling and didn't know if I would be able to afford it but was going to make it happen. Well, I ended up having to cancel the trip and getting a refund to use the funds to keep my car from being repossessed and my insurance from canceling.

At first, I was disappointed and upset because I was supposed to have help and didn't, and once again, I was having to sacrifice something that I wanted to take care of something that was a result of someone else's actions. But then, I had to see the situation for what it was. Even though I didn't cause the issue, I blame myself for not being in a better position financially to not be in such dire need. I had to be an adult and handle my business, even if that meant canceling my trip. The bright side was that the funds from the trip were enough to cover the bills that I needed paid, and I didn't have to call anyone to borrow any money. Thank you Spirit! I'm grateful that I was able to make a way out of that mess. I'm not dwelling on the fact that I may not take my trip. I'm rejoicing in the fact that I still have a car to drive to get my family back and forth. I'm at peace with the decision because it had to be done and there is no point in beating myself up over it. What's done is done and who knows, I still have a few months before my birthday. Spirit may just bless me with that trip after all.

But I'm sharing this story with you to share with you how important gratitude has become in my life. The more I appreciate the things I have and the opportunities that are offered to me, the better I feel, and Spirit sends more my way.

Gratitude is seeing a situation for what it is and being accepting of the outcome. It is understanding that life isn't happening to you; it's just happening. We can all complain and vent about all the things we don't have that we want or need, but life becomes a little sweeter when you see the things you do have and realize that things are not as bad as they seem.

We all want more and if we could just snap our fingers, we would have all the things we think we need. Imagine for a moment that someone is praying for the things you have. That car that you hate, someone would be grateful to have a way to get back and forth. That apartment that you feel is too small or too hood, someone sleeping on the street would love to have a roof over their head. Those old clothes hanging in your closet, someone would dream of having more than one outfit to wear.

When I started to look at things differently, I felt a major energy shift. I wasn't as stressed. My blood pressure was leveling out. I started to have fun again, but most importantly, I started to really appreciate what I had and that made life so much easier. It didn't take away all the burdens, but I was able to handle them with grace and ease. I was loving the life that I had built and was excited to see what was coming in the future. I don't remember the last time I smiled as much as I do now. My husband is amazing. My kids are amazing, and damn it, I'm freaking amazing!! And I give thanks for that daily because I know that no matter what comes our way, Spirit always has our back and I'm so thankful for that.

The "Smile"

Oh, the smile. The best form of makeup you could ever wear. It covers the imperfections-those we see and those we can't, but it also transforms.

We've all seen the makeup videos. In the beginning of the video, the person is usually looking a hot mess. Then, they start applying all this stuff to their face and next thing you know, a totally different person appears on the screen. Or how about when you're out running some errands with a million things on your mind, and there's some random person just smiling and enjoying life, and they manage to make eye contact with you. Now, you're smiling and everything you were just thinking about fades into the background. That's the power of a smile.

I was literally dying on the inside. So many hurts and pains had taken over every moment of my waking life. I felt like I was trapped in a room that was slowly losing air. My finances were a mess. My marriage was falling apart. Hell, even the way I carried myself had changed. I had become timid and self-conscious. A mere shell of the outgoing woman I used to be, but just like an actress, when life said "action," I would turn on the smile.

The smile to me was like the bars to a prison. It kept the bad from getting out while also keeping any good from getting in. As long as people saw me smile, they couldn't see the turmoil slowly brewing on the inside. Remember, I'm the "Strong" one. No one could tear down these brick walls that I've spent years building. No one could do it. Not even me. But one day, everything changed.

I was mindlessly scrolling on social media, and I saw this video. The video was talking about how hard it is for most people to look at themselves in the mirror and say, “I love you.” My first thought was this is crazy. Of course I love me, and guess what I did? I trotted my big, bad self over to the bathroom mirror, looked myself straight in the eyes, and froze. I was like a deer in headlights. The words were there. I knew I loved me. So, why couldn’t I say it?

When I looked in the mirror, I didn't recognize the person staring back at me. All I could see was the shame, the guilt, the rejection, the fear, the love handles, the stress bumps, and everything else I thought was wrong with me. Oh, and did I mention the smile? Sitting in its rightful place but sticking out like a cactus in a bed of roses. It just didn't belong.

I couldn't believe it. How could I expect anyone else to love me when I didn't love me? Me? The person who she spent her whole life protecting and shielding from the ugliness of life. The person she carried the burden for even when it was too much to bear. The person she showed up for when she couldn't show up for herself. The person she sacrificed her life for so that I would get to enjoy mine.

From that day forward, I vowed to love her just as much as she has loved me for the past 40 years. I thank her for looking out for me and always having my best interest at heart. I appreciate her for going through the fire for me. I ask her to forgive me for taking her for granted and not showing her the love and kindness she deserves. I love her.

Every day, I look in the mirror and I see her, but now, I know her. She is me and baby, I love me! And that beautiful smile that we've always had is exactly where it should be.

Chapter 40

Yes, honey!! I'm so proud of how far you have come, but I'm even more excited to see how much further you will go. We've always dreamed of this day and here we are living it. It hasn't always been easy, but it has absolutely been worth it. Breathe it all in. Allow yourself to be present and feel, really feel, this moment. Soak in this feeling. Express gratitude and celebrate. Truly celebrate because you deserve it. All the long nights, the tears, the heartache have all been for this moment.

This is your time to shine. Let that light that you used to hide blind everyone in your space. You are the star of the show and baby, you've earned it. You put in the work. You! This moment is all about you. All the love is for you. All the support is for you. All the happiness is for you, but most importantly, that beautiful smile is all for you.

So, here's to 40 my love. May the next 40 years be filled with more healing, more growth, more money, more happiness and all the love your big ole heart can hold.

Happy Birthday!!

I Love You Forever and Always,
-Shirley

The "Curse Breaker"

This wasn't a part of the original manuscript. As I was I getting the book finished, Spirit told me the book wasn't done. I had shared my struggles and how I coped, but I left out the most important piece of the puzzle. The why. Why all the struggles? The pain? The heavy loads? Why me?

For 40 years, I've been asking, "Why me?" And for 40 years, the answer has always been, "Why not you?" Like many of you, I cried and prayed for things to be just a little bit easier, and every time, they seemed to get harder. I couldn't understand it. Until now. Also, like many of you, I pray for my kids to not have to experience the things that I did, and unfortunately, that's not entirely up to you, or is it?

So many people talk about generational curses and breaking generational curses, but do they really understand how deep that goes? If your lineage had 100 years of karmic debt and curses that has not been cleared, and you were put here to clear the debt, do you think that life would be all sunshine and rainbows? Absolutely not! Life is going to be hard and then, add in the debt that you may collect along the way. You may start to wonder, "Can this be done in this lifetime?" Absolutely!

For as long as I can remember, I've had to struggle with something, but the last 12 years have been enough to make me want to throw in the towel. However, no matter how hard things were, I continued to push through. I didn't know why. I just knew I had to.

Oh, but now! Now, I know that I am the curse breaker. The debt is being repaid, and future generations will be operating in the black. No more repaying a debt that they don't owe. They are free to live their lives on their terms, and I couldn't be happier.

At the end of the day, the struggles were a part of my destiny. I am grateful for the opportunity to change not only my life, but the lives of my children and generations to come. I am the curse breaker. It all stops with me.

Resources

"The Black Woman's Ultimate Guide to Reclaiming Femininity" by Six the Goddis

"The Four Agreements" by Don Miguel Ruiz

"Please" & "Pussy Prayers" by Black Girl Bliss

"The Prosperity Bible: The Greatest Writings of All Time on the Secrets to Wealth and Prosperity" by Napoleon Hill, Benjamin Franklin, James Allen, Wallace D. Wattles, Ernest Holmes, Florence Scovel Shinn, and others

"You Are A Bad Ass at Making Money" by Jen Sincero

"Learning to D.A.N.C.E. With Your Demons: A Guide to Self Transformation" by Francesca Flood Ed.D.

Join us on Facebook!!
www.facebook.com/therealinceptionpublishing

www.ingramcontent.com/pod-product-compliance
Lightning Source LLC
Chambersburg PA
CBHW072127090426
42739CB00012B/3089
* 9 7 8 1 7 3 7 9 2 7 3 3 4 *